It's a Scandal!

and other sketches

Derek Haylock

The National Society
*Leading Education
with a Christian Purpose*
Church House Publishing

National Society/Church House Publishing
Church House
Great Smith Street
London SW1P 3NZ

ISBN 0 7151 4974 1

Published 2002 by National Society Enterprises Ltd

Cover design by 3t creative

Printed in England by Halstan & Co. Ltd., Amersham, Bucks.

CONTENTS

INTRODUCTION

It's a Scandal! is a collection of scripts intended for those looking for pieces of Bible-based drama that involve a good number of performers, such as a class of youngsters in a school or a church youth group. In writing and assembling this material I have tried as far as possible to ensure that each sketch satisfies the following criteria:

* it should communicate a clear, Bible-based, Christian message;

* it should involve at least twelve performers, and, if possible, any other available performers who want to take part in some capacity;

* there should be some opportunities for those with very limited acting and speaking skills to participate; and

* the demands of the material should recognize that those who might use it are likely to have only limited rehearsal time available.

Readers will find that most of the sketches therefore require just a few good performers with some acting talent. In addition, they make extensive use of narrators, extras, choruses and so on. Some of these pieces are particularly suited for children, others for older young people, and some would be most effective with a mixture of adults and children. But I have decided not to indicate which category each sketch comes into in my own mind. This is because I have found in the past that adult drama groups have sometimes put on successfully material that I had intended for young people, and vice versa.

Quotations from scripture are taken from the NIV (The Holy Bible, New International Version, New York International Bible Society; 1984 British version). These quotations are usually verbatim, but occasionally I have had to edit them slightly for the purpose of the drama, without, I hope, distorting the meaning.

Please feel free to adapt these scripts to your own circumstances, modify them, improve them, as you wish, without reference to me, provided that the clear Christian message contained in each one is retained.

This collection is being published along with a companion volume, *One Cool Cat and other sketches*, written to the same criteria.

It is always encouraging to get feedback from those who use my material, so please let me know how you get on with *It's a Scandal!* You can contact me via the publisher or by email on d.haylock@uea.ac.uk.

Derek Haylock
Norwich

FORETOLD, FULFILLED

A dramatized reading for Christmas or Easter

Introduction

This dramatized reading was a response to a request from the Methodist churches of Chorley to come up with a longer sketch based on an earlier piece called 'Rejection' (in *Plays on the Word*, National Society/Church House Publishing, 1993). It uses the same central idea of there being no room for Christ at Bethlehem and his rejection at Calvary. But here the piece goes on to the resurrection and shows how the birth, life, death and resurrection of Jesus were all fulfilments of what was foretold by the prophets in the Old Testament. For the dramatized reading, all the text, spoken by two prophets and a reader, is taken from the Bible. This is topped and tailed by a short prelude and an even shorter postlude which illustrate the idea that 'the stone the builders have rejected has become the chief capstone'. Apart from the very brief dialogue involved in the prelude and postlude there are no lines to learn, only actions. A total of 18 performers is required.

Bible base   Hebrews 1.1-2; Jeremiah 23.5-6; Isaiah 60.1-2; Haggai 2.6-7; Isaiah 9.2; Zechariah 9.9; Isaiah 11.1-3; 28.16-17; 11.4-5; John 1.1-5; 3.19; Micah 5.2; Isaiah 7.14; Luke 2.4-7; Isaiah 9.6-7; John 1.9-11; Isaiah 53.3,7-8; John 19.18; Isaiah 53.5,10; Psalm 16.10-11; Isaiah 53.11; Psalm 118.22-3; 1 Peter 2.4-8.
(Note: for dramatic purposes I have had to do some minor editing of the Bible text here and there, without, I hope, at any stage altering the underlying meaning and significance.)

Cast   Builders 1, 2 and 3 (*in modern-day dress*) for the Prelude and Postlude
Reader
Prophet A (*representing various Old Testament prophets*)
Prophet B (*representing Isaiah*)
Nine 'citizens'
Mary
Joseph
The adult Jesus

Mary and Joseph should be in costume. The adult Jesus should be clearly identifiable as such. The Reader is amplified, off-stage and not seen. The two Prophets should be positioned separately off-stage, on opposite sides, but visible when in the spotlight. They should be dressed as Old Testament characters. When they speak they are picked out by spotlights. They can read their lines from scrolls, but should deliver their prophecies forcefully and as though with the authority of God!

At the start, seated in the dark, the group of nine 'citizens' is spread randomly over the stage. They could be dressed simply in black modern-day clothes. The movements of the citizens should be carefully rehearsed, so that their gestures and postures are synchronized. Some suggestions for appropriate gestures are made below, but there is scope for your own interpretation here, to make their responses to the text as dramatic and overt as possible. The music of 'O little town of Bethlehem', 'There is a green hill' and 'Thine be the glory' is required. This could be played live on a keyboard or pre-recorded. The stage requires a short ramp or steps leading up to a raised platform at the back centre-stage. The success of this piece will depend on the effectiveness of the lighting.

Dialogue		Stage directions
Prelude		
		The stage is in darkness.
		Spotlight onto one corner of the stage.
		Two builders enter into the light. One is
		pushing a wheelbarrow full of stones.
Builder 1	This one? Yes?	*They stop and examine three stones,*
Builder 2	Yes. This one? Yes?	*picking them up one by one and then*
Builder 1	Yes. This one? Yes?	*putting them back in the wheelbarrow.*
Builder 2	Yes. This one? No?	*Their examination of the stones and*
Builder 1	No.	*decision-making should be very*
Builder 2	Reject?	*exaggerated and humorous.*
Builder 1	Yes.	*A fourth stone is then examined,*
		rejected and left on the corner of the stage.
		They exit.
		Spotlight off. Stage returns to darkness.
Dramatized reading		
Reader	In the past God spoke to our forefathers through the prophets at many times and in various ways, but in these last days he has spoken to us by his Son, whom he appointed heir of all things, and through whom he made the universe.	*The voice of the Reader is heard.*

Prophet A	'The days are coming', declares the Lord, 'when I will raise up to David a righteous Branch, a King who will reign wisely and do what is just and right in the land. This is the name by which he will be called: The Lord Our Righteousness.'	*Spotlight on Prophet A.* *Spotlight off Prophet A.*
Prophet B	Arise, shine, for your light has come, and the glory of the Lord rises upon you. See, darkness covers the earth and thick darkness is over the peoples, but the Lord rises upon you and his glory appears over you.	*Spotlight on Prophet B.* *The stage lights come up gradually. The citizens look round and gradually stand.* *Spotlight off Prophet B.*
Prophet A	This is what the Lord Almighty says: 'In a little while I will once more shake the heavens and the earth, the sea and the dry land. I will shake all nations, and the one who is desired by all nations will come, and I will fill this house with glory,' says the Lord Almighty.	*Spotlight on Prophet A.* *The citizens slowly turn to listen to Prophet A, cupping their right hands to their ears.* *Spotlight off Prophet A.*
Prophet B	The people walking in darkness have seen a great light; on those living in the land of the shadow of death a light has dawned.	*Spotlight on Prophet B.* *The citizens turn and take a few steps towards Prophet B, raise heads expectantly and hold out arms in a welcoming, worshipful gesture.* *Spotlight off Prophet B.*
Prophet A	Rejoice greatly, O Daughter of Zion! Shout, Daughter of Jerusalem! See, your king comes to you, righteous and bringing salvation.	*Spotlight on Prophet A.* *Citizens turn, move quickly towards Prophet A; they adopt an excited, expectant pose.* *Spotlight off Prophet A.*

Prophet B	A shoot will come up from the stump of Jesse; from his roots a Branch will bear fruit. The Spirit of the Lord will rest on him . . . – the Spirit of wisdom and of understanding – the Spirit of counsel and of power – the Spirit of knowledge and of the fear of the Lord – and he will delight in the fear of the Lord.	*Spotlight on Prophet B.* *The citizens turn and move quickly across towards Prophet B, but as he speaks they begin to look doubtful.* *They take a step back to coincide with each of these four phrases, backing away from Prophet B.* *Spotlight off Prophet B.*
Prophet A	So this is what the Sovereign Lord says: 'See, I lay a stone in Zion, a tested stone, a precious cornerstone for a sure foundation; the one who trusts will never be dismayed. I will make justice the measuring line . . . and righteousness the plumb-line.'	*Spotlight on Prophet A.* *The citizens turn towards Prophet A, listening.* *Now they adopt a pose suggesting resistance to the message.* *Spotlight off Prophet A.*
Prophet B	With righteousness he will judge the needy. With justice he will give decisions for the poor of the earth. He will strike the earth with the rod of his mouth. With the breath of his lips he will slay the wicked. Righteousness will be his belt . . . and faithfulness the sash round his waist.	*Spotlight on Prophet B.* *The citizens look towards Prophet B. They turn away from him defiantly, arms folded.* *They look towards Prophet B again.* *They turn away and mime indignation, arms akimbo.* *They look towards Prophet B again.* *They turn away and put their fingers in their ears.* *Spotlight off Prophet B.*
Reader	In the beginning was the Word, and the Word was with God, and the Word was God. He was with God in the beginning. Through him all things	*Citizens freeze.* *The Reader's voice is heard off-stage.*

were made; without him nothing was made that has been made. In him was life, and that life was the light of men. The light shines in the darkness, but the darkness has not understood it. This is the verdict: light has come into the world, but people loved darkness instead of light because their deeds were evil.

Gradually, the stage lights go down, as the citizens one by one relax, drift away and exit, stage left.

Stage now in darkness.

Prophet A But you, Bethlehem Ephrathah, though you are small among the clans of Judah, out of you will come for me one who will be ruler over Israel, whose origins are from of old, from ancient times.

Spotlight on Prophet A.

Spotlight off Prophet A.

Stage lights come up, as the music of 'O little town' fades in; citizens march on slowly, carrying placards; they form a straight line across the middle of the stage. As one by one they turn to face the audience, the placards are seen to spell out BETHLEHEM.

Prophet B Therefore the Lord himself will give you a sign: a virgin will be with child and will give birth to a son, and will call him Immanuel.

Spotlight on Prophet B.

Spotlight off Prophet B.

Reader Joseph went up from the town of Nazareth in Galilee to Judaea, to Bethlehem the town of David, because he belonged to the house and line of David.
He went there to register with Mary, who was

Mary and Joseph enter stage right, he assisting her in an anxious and caring manner.
Mary and Joseph head towards the line of citizens. The one on the extreme right of the line takes one pace to the right, thus making a gap in the line. As Mary and Joseph move to go through this gap the next citizen takes a pace to the right

pledged to be married to him and was expecting a child.
While they were there, the time came for the baby to be born.
But there was no room for them in the inn.
And she gave birth to her firstborn, a son. She wrapped him in cloths and placed him in a manger, because there was no room for them in the inn.

and closes it. This then opens up a new gap in the line, which in turn is closed by the next citizen. So, as Mary and Joseph make their way along the line, each gap that opens to them is closed. As each citizen moves they turn their placard round to reveal messages written on the reverse side: NO ROOM; SORRY; FULL UP; TRY ELSEWHERE; NO VACANCIES; NOT HERE; APOLOGIES; TOO BUSY; PACKED OUT. Finally, Mary and Joseph slowly walk away and exit stage left.
Music fades and stops.
The citizens turn their backs towards the audience. One citizen from the end of the line collects all the placards and exits. The others go down on one knee as they hand over their placards. They hold this position.

Prophet B To us a child is born, to us a son is given. And he will be called Wonderful Counsellor, Mighty God, Everlasting Father, Prince of Peace. He will reign on David's throne and over his kingdom, establishing and upholding it with justice and righteousness for ever.

Spotlight on Prophet B.

Spotlight off Prophet B.
The stage lights go down.

Reader The true light that gives light to every man was coming into the world. He was in the world, and though the world was made through him, the world did not recognize him. He came to that which was his own, but his own did not receive him.

In the darkness, the adult Jesus enters and stands behind the citizens, with his hands held out in a gesture of invitation.
The lights gradually come up again to reveal him standing there.

The citizens stand slowly and turn to face Jesus.

Music of 'There is a green hill' begins.

Prophet B   He was despised and rejected by men, a man of sorrows, and familiar with suffering. Like one from whom men hide their faces he was despised, and we esteemed him not. He was oppressed and afflicted, yet he did not open his mouth; he was led like a lamb to the slaughter; and as a sheep before her shearers is silent, so he did not open his mouth. By oppression and judgement he was taken away.

Spotlight on Prophet B.
The citizens now turn their backs on Jesus again.

They walk slowly backwards, pushing Jesus up the ramp as Prophet B continues.

Spotlight off Prophet B.

Jesus is now on the platform. He turns his back on the audience.

Reader   They crucified him.

Simultaneously: music stops abruptly; stage lights go down; spotlight on Jesus; he snaps into a crucified posture; the citizens freeze. There is a loud drumbeat, then silence for about ten seconds.

Prophet B   But he was pierced for our transgressions, he was crushed for our iniquities; the punishment that brought us peace was upon him, and by his wounds we are healed. Yet it was the Lord's will to crush him and to cause him to suffer.

Spotlight on Prophet B.
The citizens walk off slowly, either side.

Jesus falls to the floor of the platform and lies there, still.

Silence for about ten seconds.

Prophet A   But you, O God, will not abandon him to the grave, nor will you let your Holy One see decay. You have made known to him the path of life.

Spotlight on Prophet A.
The music of 'Thine be the glory' fades in. Jesus stands, and walks confidently down the ramp.

Prophet B   After the suffering of his soul, he will see the light of life and be satisfied.

Jesus takes position centre-stage, head raised towards heaven, arms out in worship.

 — 7 —

Prophet A	The stone the builders rejected has become the capstone; the Lord has done this, and it is marvellous in our eyes.	*Spotlights off Prophets A and B.*
Reader	Come to him, the living Stone, rejected by men, but chosen by God and precious to him.	*Jesus now stands centre-stage, looks out towards the audience and opens his arms wider in a gesture of invitation. He holds this position until the music reaches an appropriate conclusion.* *Blackout.*
Postlude		*A spotlight shines on the rejected stone on the corner of the stage. Enter a third builder, who sees the stone, picks it up and examines it. He speaks his line, then exits excitedly with the stone.*
Builder 3	Well, look at this! Now, this . . . could be . . . just what I've been looking for!	*Blackout.*

QUESTIONS AND ANSWERS

For Christmas

Introduction

This sketch provides an opportunity to involve a good number of performers, by using two choruses who participate in a question-and-answer conversation. This conversation forms the backdrop to actors portraying Mary, Joseph, shepherds and wise men coming to Bethlehem.

Bible base	The account of the first Christmas, as recorded in Matthew 1 – 2, Luke 1 – 2.
Cast	Two Choruses, Q and A, with about five or six in each Angel (*an off-stage, amplified voice*) Mary, Joseph, Shepherds, three Wise Men (*in traditional costumes*) One performer to act as a signpost Stagehands, to bring on the manger and the stable and to hold up the stable

The performer acting as a signpost stands at the back of the stage, with back turned to the audience. This performer has three signs (BETHLEHEM; ON A HILLSIDE: IN THE DESERT), which are hidden, but will be used later to identify the location of the action. The two Choruses are off-stage, one each side. Chorus Q asks questions, which Chorus A answers. They may read their lines from scripts, but it is essential that the conversation flows quickly backwards and forwards between them without breaks.

Chorus Q	Where are we?
	(*Signpost turns to face the audience and displays the sign saying BETHLEHEM.*)
Chorus A	Can't you read?
Chorus Q	Bethlehem?
Chorus A	In Judaea.
	(*Two stagehands bring on a stable outline and hold it up in place.*)
Chorus Q	What's that?
Chorus A	A stable.
	(*Stagehand enters and places a manger and two small stools in front of the stable outline.*)
Chorus Q	And what's that?
Chorus A	A manger.
Chorus Q	What's it for?

☹ —9— ☺

(*Mary and Joseph enter. She is carrying a baby.*)

Chorus A	Feeding animals.
Chorus Q	Who are they?
Chorus A	Joseph. And Mary.

(*Joseph and Mary sit.*)

Chorus Q	They look exhausted.
Chorus A	Long journey.
Chorus Q	Where from?
Chorus A	Nazareth. Up north.

(*Mary places the baby in the manger.*)

Chorus Q	Is that a baby?
Chorus A	You're catching on!
Chorus Q	In a manger?
Chorus A	All they could find.
Chorus Q	In a stable?
Chorus A	No room in the inn.
Chorus Q	Boy or girl?
Mary	It's a boy.
Chorus Q	What will you call him?
Angel	(*Off-stage, amplified*) Name him Jesus.
Chorus Q	Who said that?
Chorus A	An angel from heaven.
Joseph	In my dream.
Mary	Name him Jesus.
Joseph	So we did.

(*Mary picks up the baby and holds him in her arms.*)

Mary	We named him Jesus.
Joseph	Saviour of the world.
Chorus Q	Is he someone special then?
Angel	He will be called the Son of God.
Chorus Q	Who said that?
Chorus A	An angel from heaven.
Chorus Q	The Son of God? In a manger?
Chorus A	In a stable.
Chorus Q	Just a baby?
Chorus A	It's what God promised.
Mary	A virgin will bear a son.

(*Mary hands the baby to Joseph.*)

Joseph	And he will be called 'Emmanuel'.
Mary	God with us.

(*Signpost changes to ON A HILLSIDE; Shepherds enter and sit on the floor, away from the manger.*)

☹ — 10 — ☺

Chorus Q	Where are we now?
Chorus A	Can't you read?
Chorus Q	On a hillside?
Chorus A	Outside Bethlehem.
Chorus Q	Who are they?
Chorus A	Shepherds, of course.
Angel	Good news! Great joy!
	(Shepherds respond to Angel's voice, looking up in wonder, surprise, fear.)
Chorus Q	Who said that?
Chorus A	An angel from heaven.
Chorus Q	Might have guessed!
Angel	The Saviour is born in Bethlehem.
	(One Shepherd stands, excited.)
Shepherd	Let's go at once!
	(Other Shepherds stand and act as though discussing which way to go.)
Chorus Q	Where are they going?
Chorus A	Can't you guess?
Chorus Q	Bethlehem?
Chorus A	You're catching on!
	(Shepherds start to move towards the stable.)
Chorus Q	They're rather scruffy.
Chorus A	Not very bright.
	(Shepherds stop and look in turn at the two Choruses, as if offended by what they say.)
Chorus Q	Smell of sheep.
Chorus A	So, what's your point?
Chorus Q	Going to see the Son of God?
Chorus A	Saviour of the world!
	(Joseph hands the baby back to Mary and stands. Shepherds move towards the stable.)
Chorus Q	Will they be welcome?
Chorus A	Watch. And learn.
	(Shepherds arrive at the stable. Joseph and Mary greet them. They position themselves standing around the back of the manger. The signpost changes to IN THE DESERT.)
Chorus Q	Where are we now?
	(Wise Men enter, looking around them, up into the sky, consulting maps and so on, as the conversation goes on.)
Chorus A	Can't you read?
Chorus Q	In the dessert?
Chorus A	In the desert!
Chorus Q	Who are they?
Chorus A	Three wise men.

☹ — 11 — ☺

Chorus Q	Where are they from?
Wise Man	We come from the East.
Chorus Q	Where are you going?
Chorus A	Can't you guess?
Chorus Q	Bethlehem?
Wise Men	You're catching on!
Chorus Q	How do they know . . . ?
Chorus A	Where to go? Can't you guess?
Chorus Q	An angel from heaven!
Chorus A	Sorry, no. They followed a star.
	(*Wise Men now act as though spotting the star again and start to move off. They may need to go off-stage and come back on again, depending on timing and space available.*)
Chorus Q	They look very rich!
Chorus A	They're very clever.
Chorus Q	They look so important.
Chorus A	So, what's your point?
Chorus Q	Going so far to see a baby?
Chorus A	Just a tiny newborn child.
Chorus Q	Born in a stable?
Chorus A	Laid in a manger.
	(*Wise Men now arrive at the stable.*)
Chorus Q	Will they be welcome?
Chorus A	Watch. And learn.
	(*Joseph and Mary greet them. The Wise Men remain standing.*)
Chorus Q	So shepherds came.
Chorus A	Came to Jesus.
Chorus Q	And they were welcome.
	(*Shepherds kneel in worship.*)
Chorus A	They understood.
Chorus Q	And wise men came.
Chorus A	Came to Jesus.
Chorus Q	And they were welcome.
	(*Wise Men kneel and present their gifts.*)
Chorus A	They understood.
Chorus Q	So . . .
Chorus A	Yes . . . ?
Chorus Q	Can anyone come?
Chorus A	What, come to Jesus?
Chorus Q	Would *we* be welcome?
All except Chorus Q	You're catching on!

OH DEAR, YOU MISSED THEM!

For Christmas

Introduction

This sketch imagines the traditional three Wise Men going to Bethlehem, accompanied by a fourth, not-so-wise colleague. He gets distracted by many things on the way and ends up missing the opportunity to meet the Christ-child. There is an obvious implied parallel with the way in which we too can be so distracted by the trivial non-essentials of Christmas that we fail to come face to face with the Lord Jesus, who should be at the centre of it all. The sketch requires four good actors who can learn a substantial number of lines to play the parts of the Wise Men, plus a number of players who have walk-on parts with a few simple lines.

Bible base	Matthew 2.1-12; Numbers 24.17.
Cast	The traditional 'three Wise Men', plus a fourth, who is, in fact, not-so-wise
	Sellers 1–6
	Herod
	A group of chief priests and teachers of the law (*including two speaking parts*)
	A citizen of Jerusalem
	Narrator (*off-stage*)

The 'three Wise Men' enter, consulting their maps and the stars.

Wise Man 1	(*Pointing*) Look! Have you seen the star?
Wise Man 2	Is it a sign from God?
Wise Man 3	Could this be the day we've been waiting for?
Wise Man 1	See, here in the ancient scriptures . . .
	(*They look together at an old document.*)
Wise Man 2	(*Reading*) 'I see him, but not now; I behold him, but not near. A star will come out of Jacob; a sceptre will rise out of Israel.'
Wise Man 3	Is it time to go? To Jerusalem?
	(*The fourth Wise Man enters in a hurry from stage left.*)
Wise Man 4	Hi there, guys! Sorry I'm late. They had a sale at Ali's Emporium. Did you see their offers on Wise Men's outfits? No? Oh dear, you missed them! Typical! You always miss the best things. Look, I got my new gear there. (*Showing off outfit*) You like it? Cool, eh? Are these

sleeves generous, or what? Just feel that quality. (*Realizing the others are not interested*) Sorry, what's going on then?

Wise Man 1	Look, the star . . . (*pointing*)
Wise Man 2	The one who is promised has been born . . . (*pointing to the book*)
Wise Man 3	We must go to him at once . . . (*pointing off-stage right*)
Wise Man 4	Right. OK. With you, guys.
Wise Man 1	We should take gifts for the newborn King.
Wise Man 4	Right, gifts.

(*Wise Man 4 exits stage left to collect a gift. The others pick up their gifts from somewhere on stage.*)

Wise Man 1	I will take gold. Gold for a King.
Wise Man 2	I will take frankincense. A thank-offering to God.
Wise Man 3	I will take myrrh. Because he must suffer.

(*Enter Wise Man 4 from stage left, bearing his gift – a Teletubby doll!*)

Wise Man 4	And I will take . . . a Teletubby!

(*The others look exasperated!*)

Wise Man 1	Have you any idea what is going on here?
Wise Man 2	Can you imagine what it will sound like in years to come when people read about the birth of the promised saviour?
Wise Man 3	(*As if quoting*) 'And when they had opened their treasures, they presented unto him gifts: gold, and frankincense, and myrrh . . . and a Tinky-winky.' Honestly!
Wise Man 1	Come on, let's get going.
Wise Man 2	Follow the star!
Wise Man 3	To Jerusalem!

(*They gather up their gifts, maps and so on, and set off. To represent the journey they should go off-stage right, wait off-stage for a while, then make their way slowly in front of the stage and enter again from stage left. This will happen a number of times, the fourth Wise Man getting delayed each time by people who enter from stage right just after the others have left.*)

Narrator	After Jesus was born in Bethlehem in Judaea, during the time of King Herod, wise men from the east came to Jerusalem.
Wise Man 4	(*Being a bit slow gathering his things together*) OK . . . right . . . just coming . . . (*Starts to exit.*)

(*Enter Sellers 1 and 2, bearing appropriate items. Wise Man 4 stops and gets interested when he hears them calling.*)

Seller 1	(*Calling out*) Everything you need for your journey across the desert. Buy it here. Sunshades, suncream, sundials.
Seller 2	Best prices. Sandals, sandwiches, sandpaper. The *Rough Guide to the Arabian Desert.*
Wise Man 4	Ooh, yes please. I'll have one of those sunshades and . . . a pair of sandals.

> *(He pays for and collects his purchases. The Sellers exit stage left, as Wise Man 4 starts to set off to catch up the others. Wise Man 1 appears from stage right.)*

Wise Man 1   Are you coming?

Wise Man 4   Yes, yes . . . but did you see those guys selling stuff for the desert?

Wise Man 1   No, we didn't. We're trying to get to Jerusalem!

Wise Man 4   *(Catching up)* Oh dear, you missed them. Typical! You always miss the best things.

> *(They exit and continue on their journey. Sellers 3 and 4 enter stage right, with a box of Christmas wrapping-paper. The Wise Men come on from stage left. The first three ignore the sellers and exit stage right. The fourth stops when he hears them calling and gets drawn in.)*

Seller 3   Best wrapping-paper!

Seller 4   Lovely designs!

Seller 3   Six sheets a shekel!

Seller 4   Just what you need for wrapping up your gifts.

Wise Man 4   That looks a bargain. I'll have six sheets, please. Thank you.

> *(He makes his purchase and the sellers exit stage left. Wise Man 1 appears from stage right.)*

Wise Man 1   Are you coming?

Wise Man 4   Yes, yes . . . but didn't you see those guys selling this great wrapping-paper?

Wise Man 1   No, we didn't. We're trying to get to Jerusalem!

Wise Man 4   *(Catching up)* Oh dear, you missed them. Typical! You always miss the best things.

> *(They exit and continue on their journey. Seller 5 enters stage right, with a Christmas tree, followed by Seller 6 with Christmas decorations. The Wise Men come on from stage left. The first three Wise Men ignore the sellers and exit stage right. The fourth stops when he hears them calling and gets drawn in.)*

Seller 5   Get your festive tree here! Best quality.

Wise Man 4   Festive tree? What do you do with that, then?

Seller 5   You . . . er . . . put it in your living-room, sir.

Wise Man 4   And then what?

Seller 6   You . . . er . . . cover it with decorations, sir.

Wise Man 4   And then what?

Seller 5   Well, that's it, really.

Seller 6   Until all the needles drop off. Then you throw it away.

Seller 5   But everyone has one at this time of the year, sir.

Wise Man 4   Well . . . OK then. I'd better have one.

Seller 5   *(Making sale)* There you are, sir. Twenty-five shekels. Thank you.

Seller 6   *(Making sale)* And a starter pack of decorations. That's another twenty-five shekels. Thank you.

Wise Man 4   Right. Thanks.

(The sellers exit stage left. Wise Man 1 appears from stage right.)

Wise Man 1 Are you coming?

Wise Man 4 Yes, yes . . . but didn't you see those guys selling these festive trees? Apparently, you cover them with decorations and put them in your living-room.

Wise Man 1 No, we didn't. We're trying to get to Jerusalem!

Wise Man 4 *(Catching up)* Oh dear, you missed them. Typical! You always miss the best things.

(They exit and continue on their journey, while the Narrator reads the passage below. Wise Man 4 is getting increasingly cluttered with all his purchases.)

Narrator The wise men from the east came to Jerusalem and asked, 'Where is the one who has been born king of the Jews? We saw his star in the east and have come to worship him.' When King Herod heard this he was disturbed, and all Jerusalem with him. He called together all the chief priests and teachers of the law.

(Enter Herod stage right, chief priests and teachers of the law stage left.)

Herod Where is the Christ to be born?

Teacher 1 In Bethlehem in Judaea, your majesty.

Teacher 2 This is what the prophet has written: *(reading)* 'for out of you, Bethlehem, will come a ruler who will be the shepherd of my people Israel.'

(The priests and teachers of the law bow and exit.)

Narrator Then Herod called the wise men secretly and found out from them the exact time the star had appeared.

(Enter Wise Men 1–3 stage left, with appropriate action.)

Herod Go to Bethlehem and make a careful search for the child. As soon as you find him, report to me, *(slightly sinister)* so that I too may go and worship him.

Narrator After they had heard the king, they went on their way, and the star they had seen in the east went ahead of them.

(Herod exits stage left. Wise Men start to exit stage right.)

Wise Man 1 Let us go at once.

Wise Man 2 To Bethlehem.

Wise Man 3 *(Pointing)* Look! The star!

(They exit stage right, passing the Citizen entering at the same time. This time they stay off-stage, without proceeding to the other side of the stage. Wise Man 4 enters from stage left, struggling with all his baggage.)

Wise Man 4 *(Addressing the Citizen)* Oh, excuse me. Have you seen three wise guys around here anywhere? Kind of oriental-looking? Searching for a newborn king? Going on about a star?

Citizen Oh, yes. I think I just passed them. Heading off towards Bethlehem. *(Pointing stage right)* Bethlehem is that way.

Wise Man 4 Thanks. Right, I'll just get some provisions and then I'll follow them. Where's the nearest supermarket?

Citizen	(*Pointing stage left*) The supermarket is that way. I'll show you. I'm going there myself. (*Chatting excitedly as they exit together*) They've got fresh turkeys at half-price; mince pies, buy one get one free; twenty per cent off their walnuts . . . (*Both exit stage left.*)
Narrator	The star stopped over the place where the child was. When they saw the star, the wise men were overjoyed. On coming to the house, they saw the child with his mother Mary, and they bowed down and worshipped him. Then they opened their treasures and presented him with gifts of gold and of incense and of myrrh. And having been warned in a dream not to go back to Herod, they returned to their country by another route. (*Wise Man 4 enters from stage left, now carrying, in addition to everything else, some full carrier bags from a well-known supermarket chain. Wise Men 1–3 enter from stage right, now without their gifts.*)
Wise Man 1	We saw the child!
Wise Man 2	The newborn king!
Wise Man 3	And his mother Mary!
Wise Man 1	And we bowed down before him!
Wise Man 2	And we worshipped him!
Wise Man 3	And we gave him our gifts!
Wise Man 1	God has come into his world.
Wise Man 2	And we have met him.
Wise Man 3	Come, we must return. It is not safe for us to be here. Herod will kill the young child if he finds out where he is. (*They start to exit stage right.*)
Wise Man 4	(*Suddenly sounding in earnest*) But, wait! I haven't seen the child. And his mother. The star. Bethlehem.
Wise Man 1	Oh dear . . . you missed them!
Wise Man 2	Typical!
Wise Man 3	You always miss . . . the *best* things. (*The three Wise Men exit in a hurry, leaving Wise Man 4 on his own, looking disappointed and forlorn. Finally, he dumps all his baggage and runs off after the others.*)

Jesus is risen! Pass it on!

For Easter Sunday

Introduction

This simple dramatic idea was written as an introduction to an Easter Sunday morning service. The news about the Lord's resurrection is gradually passed around a group of disciples and then from them into and around the whole congregation, in a series of short messages, with the instruction to 'pass it on'. This is intended to lead directly into the suggested opening hymn, the great traditional Easter hymn 'Jesus Christ is risen today, alleluia!'

Bible base	John 19 – 20.
Cast	Twelve disciples: A, B, C, D, E, F, G, H, I, J, K and L A could be the person who leads the subsequent worship J and K should be male L should be female

Five players, B–F, are standing around on-stage, distributed randomly across the available area.

Message 1	The Lord is dead. Pass it on.
	(*This message is delivered in a serious tone of resignation. A enters, looking grave, and passes on message 1 to B. B goes across to C and D and repeats the message. C and D pass on the message independently to E and F. A, B and C gather together in a group.*)
Message 2	The Lord is buried. The tomb is sealed. Pass it on.
	(*This message is also delivered in a serious tone of resignation. A addresses B and C, giving them message 2. Each of the three passes on message 2 to one of D, E, and F. G, H and I enter and D, E and F pass on message 2 to them. All nine players on-stage now line up along the back of the stage, with A in the centre.*)
Message 3	It is finished.
	(*Message 3 is stated strongly by A, repeated more quietly by the two players either side of A, repeated even more quietly by the next two, and so on, until it is whispered barely audibly by the two on the ends. After delivering the line they bow their heads in turn. There is a pause and then they slowly disperse across the stage and sit, each one in isolation from the others.*)

In the subsequent messages there is a gradual crescendo of excitement. As the messages about the resurrection are passed around larger groups, eventually including the congregation, at least the first two statements of each message must be clear and distinct. The subsequent statements will then overlap and gradually become an excited babble.)

Message 4   We [*They*] went to the tomb. Pass it on.

(J and K enter and, speaking in unison, deliver message 4 ('We went . . .') to one of the players sitting on the stage. This player gets up and passes on the message to someone else ('They went . . .'). J, K and all who have received message 4 continue to pass it round, until everyone on the stage has heard it and is standing.)

Message 5   The stone was rolled away. Pass it on.

(J delivers message 5 to someone standing near J. K repeats it to someone standing near K. The message is then passed around all the players on stage.)

Message 6   The tomb was empty. Pass it on.

(K delivers message 6 to someone standing near K. J repeats it to someone standing near J. The message is then passed around all the players on stage, as with message 5.)

Message 7   I have [*She has*] seen the Lord. Pass it on.

(L enters and delivers message 7 ('I have . . .') to someone on the edge of the group. This player passes it on ('She has . . .'), and then it gets passed around the group as before, with increasing excitement. All the players on-stage now turn and face L expectantly.)

Message 8   The Lord is risen! Pass it on.

(L delivers message 8 loudly and clearly to the whole group. The whole group repeats it in unison, looking towards L for 'The Lord is risen!' and at each other for 'Pass it on'. They then run off-stage and individually pass on message 8 to twelve individuals, who have been forewarned and who are spread around the congregation.

These individuals pass on the message to the people sitting next to them. Players A–L run round the congregation, excitedly passing on the message as well, encouraging everyone to pass it on. The message should now be passed round the entire congregation, with a babble of excitement.

As the babble dies down, A goes back onto the stage. The other players stay standing around within the congregation.)

Message 9   Jesus Christ is risen today! Pass it on!

(A delivers message 9 in a strong, triumphant manner. B–L, in the congregation, repeat it to those near them. By now the congregation will have the idea and will pass the message around the church. As this is happening the piano (organ, or whatever) begins to play one verse of the hymn 'Jesus Christ is risen today'. Towards the end of this introductory verse, A announces this hymn and everyone rises to sing.)

IT's a SCANDAL!

Introduction

This is a presentation of the wonderful story of the woman who burst into the home of Simon the Pharisee and anointed the feet of Jesus with her tears and with perfume. Both her previous life and her behaviour on this occasion would have been scandalous to the Pharisees. So was the response of Jesus to the woman, in accepting her love and forgiving her sins! The sketch requires four good actors, who have the main speaking parts. But it also involves eleven others in a chorus (the panel), with a very undemanding but enjoyable contribution. The sketch portrays some kind of show, in which a panel has to decide whether some incident is or is not a scandal, indicating this by holding up cards that spell out the message: IT'S A SCANDAL.

Bible base	Luke 7.36-50.
Cast	Benny, the presenter of *It's a Scandal!*
	Simon, the Pharisee
	Nathan, one of his guests
	The Woman (*Mary*)
	Eleven members of the panel

The stage is set up with a desk and two chairs to one side. Along the back of the stage stands a line of eleven members of the panel. Each has a card, on one side of which are written large letters that will spell out IT'S A SCANDAL when they are held up. On the reverse side of the cards bearing the letters SCANDAL are written the letters MAZING plus an exclamation mark, so that later in the sketch they can be held up to display the response IT'S AMAZING! Benny enters, to a round of applause from all performers, on and off the stage, which should encourage the audience to join in as well. Benny stands centre-stage and greets the audience and the panel members.

Benny	Good evening, and good evening. Welcome, and welcome. Here we are again . . . and here we are again. For another edition of your favourite show . . .
	(*The panel members hold up their cards to display IT'S A SCANDAL.*)
Panel	(*In unison*) It's a scandal!
	(*Benny takes a seat at the desk.*)
Benny	Hello, and hello! I'm Benny, your host on *It's a Scandal!*, and this (*gesturing towards the panel*) is our lovely panel. Let's have a lovely round of applause for our lovely panel! (*He encourages the audience to applaud*) Thank you, and thank you.

Now, this evening we are investigating a case of breaking and entering at the house of Simon the Pharisee, resident of the town of Nain. And we will be asking: is it a scandal? Ladies and gentlemen, Simon the Pharisee!

(Enter Simon, who waves to the audience and the panel and takes the other seat at the desk.)

Benny   Simon, welcome, and welcome. Now, in your own words, Simon, what happened?

Simon   You know this new teacher, the one they call Jesus, from Nazareth? Well, he was in our town. So, the other evening, I invited him to a meal at my house. With some of my Pharisee friends. So we could find out more about him, discuss his ideas and so on, over dinner. Man to man.

Benny   So far, so good, Simon. So, what went wrong?

Simon   Well, suddenly, this . . . *(indicating his disgust)* woman . . . came bursting into the house. No invitation. Right in the middle of our conversation. Didn't even take her shoes off at the door. Crying her eyes out, she was. In a terrible state.

Benny   Did you recognize her? Was she a friend? An acquaintance?

Simon   I recognized her all right. But she's not a woman I would ever go near. I certainly wouldn't let her into my house! She's well known around our town, as a sinner of the lowest order. She belongs in the gutter. Disgusting!

Benny   So, panel, there's Simon's argument. A woman breaks into his house. Uninvited. Interrupts the conversation of a group of men. And she's a sinner of the worst kind. Panel . . . what is your verdict?

Panel   *(Holding up their cards to spell out IT'S A SCANDAL)* It's a scandal!

(Simon punches the air in triumph with a cry of 'Yes!' and exits.)

Benny   Yes, it's a scandal! Thank you, Simon the Pharisee. Now here is one of Simon's guests at the dinner . . . please welcome Nathan!

(Round of applause as Nathan enters, waving to the audience and the panel. He takes the seat at the desk.)

Benny   Nathan, welcome, and welcome. So, what happened next?

Nathan   It was quite appalling. This . . . *(indicating his disgust)* woman . . . this . . . sinner . . . she pushes her way through the guests . . . she actually touches me as she barges through . . . ugh! I've had to send all my clothes to be ritually cleaned.

Benny   And she was heading for Jesus, I understand. So, describe the scene.

Nathan   Well, as the guest, Jesus is lying on his side, on one of the comfy chairs, you know, resting on an elbow, with his legs stretched out. So, she goes behind him, at his feet. And she's crying and crying. And her tears are pouring onto his feet. And, would you believe it, she's drying them with her hair! And then she's got this jar of expensive perfume, right. I mean, top quality stuff. I wouldn't like to think where she got the money to pay for it. And she poured it on his feet. The whole lot. Disgraceful!

Benny	Disgraceful? Why is that?
Nathan	Well, as Simon says, if this Jesus really were a prophet, he would know what kind of woman this was, who was . . . (*outraged*) touching him . . . that she was a sinner! He should have ordered her out of the house.
Benny	Simon says, do this?
Nathan	Simon says, do that!
Benny	What does our panel think? Allowing a woman like this to touch him, to wash his feet with her tears, to anoint his feet with expensive perfume . . . panel, your verdict, please!
Panel	(*Holding up their cards to spell out IT'S A SCANDAL*) It's a scandal!
	(*Nathan raises his arms in triumph and exits.*)
Benny	Yes, it's a scandal! Thank you, Nathan. (*Seriously*) To protect her identity, we will give her the name 'Mary'. (*In a style that does not encourage applause from the audience*) Here now is the woman herself.
	(*The woman enters, nervously, looking round anxiously, and takes the seat. The panel members gasp as she enters, point towards her accusingly, mumbling under their breath.*)
	Mary, what about your behaviour that evening? Is it true what we've heard? You barged in, uninvited, into the house of a Pharisee, without even removing your shoes?
Woman	That's right, sir. Sorry, sir. It is all true.
Benny	May I see one of the shoes?
Woman	(*Hands over a sandal*) There you are, sir.
Benny	(*Holding up the sandal*) So, then, panel. What do you make of this?
	(*All the panel members except the person with C hold up their cards, to spell out IT'S A SANDAL.*)
Panel	It's a sandal!
Benny	And how did you find your way there, in the dark?
Woman	(*Getting a candle out of her pocket*) I used this, sir.
Benny	(*Turning to the panel, holding up the candle*) And what do you make of this?
	(*All the panel members except the person with S hold up their cards, to spell out IT'S A CANDAL.*)
Panel	It's a candle!
Benny	So, Mary, why did you do it? Why the tears? Why the expensive perfume on his feet?
Woman	Look, sir, I know I was a sinner. What I needed was to be forgiven. To be given a chance to start again. That's what Jesus gave me. That's why I love him so much.
Benny	But surely, only God can forgive sinners. And you say that this Jesus forgave your sins? Panel, what's your verdict on that?
Panel	(*Holding up their cards to spell out IT'S A SCANDAL*) It's a scandal!

Woman	That's what they all said. In the house. You know, all the guests. When Jesus said my sins were forgiven. They said it was a scandal. But I knew, in my heart, that it was all right now.
Benny	Now, I understand that Jesus told Simon a little story. Is that right?
Woman	Yes, sir. That's right. There were these two men who owed money to this moneylender. One owed him five hundred pounds, and the other fifty. Neither of them had the money to pay him back, so he cancelled the debts of both. Then Jesus says, 'OK, Simon, now which of them will love him more?'
Benny	And I suppose Simon replied, 'The one who had the bigger debt.'
Woman	That's right, sir. Then Jesus points to me and says: 'Do you see this woman? I came into your house. You did not give me any water for my feet, but she washed my feet with her tears and wiped them with her hair. You did not put oil on my head, but she has poured perfume on my feet. See how much she loves me? That's because her many sins have been forgiven.'
Benny	Thank you. (*Thoughtfully*) Very . . . interesting. Panel? Your final verdict . . .
	(*First, just the panel members with the cards I, T, 'S, A hold them up.*)
Panel	It's a . . . (*They hesitate; then those with the cards for S,C,A,N,D,A,L hold them up to show the reverse side: M, A, Z, I, N, G, !, spelling out IT'S AMAZING!*)
Panel	It's amazing!
Benny	Yes, indeed. Mary, it looks as though your faith has saved you. Go in peace. Goodnight, and (*to the audience*) goodnight.

THE GREAT BANQUET

Introduction

This sketch is a version of the parable that Jesus told of the great banquet in heaven. A large number of performers can take part, with parts ranging from the two lead actors and the two narrators to those who simply have walk-on parts at the end. Narrators are used to keep the action moving and to avoid too much learning of lines.

Bible base	Luke 14.15-24.
Cast	Narrators A and B
	King
	Pritstick (the King's servant)
	Four potential guests (Guests 1, 2, 3 and 4)
	Any number of poor, crippled, blind, lame and other guests

The Narrators stand on either side of the stage to deliver their lines. From the start of the sketch the four potential guests sit on a bench along the front of the stage. The opening sequence is intended to show that they are aware that the banquet will certainly be worth going to! Each guest is, however, preoccupied reading: Guest 1, a home-and-gardens style magazine; Guest 2, the Financial Times; *Guest 3, a football magazine; and Guest 4, a TV magazine. Their heads are buried in their magazines.*

Narrator A	Jesus told a story . . .
Narrator B	. . . that was something like this.
Narrator A	There once was a good, kind and mighty king . . .
Narrator B	. . . who was planning a splendid feast in his splendid palace.
Narrator A	The great day was drawing near.
	(*Enter King.*)
King	The great day is drawing near.
Narrator B	Time to make a list.
King	Pritstick!
	(*Enter Servant.*)
Servant	Yes, Your Majesty?
King	Make a list.
Servant	Yes, Sire.
	(*Servant scribbles furiously.*)

King	Now, we'll need . . . venison, sirloin, gammon and quail . . .
Guests	(*Looking up from their magazines*) Yummy!
Servant	Cabbage sandwiches?
Guests	Ugh! (*Back to their reading.*)
King	No, thank you, Pritstick! We'll have . . . aubergine, parsnip, pumpkin and truffles . . .
Guests	(*Looking up from their magazines*) Yummy! Yummy!
Servant	Spinach soup?
Guests	Ugh! (*Back to their reading.*)
King	No, thank you, Pritstick! We'll have . . . ice cream and cheesecake, gateaux and muffins . . .
Guests	(*Looking up from their magazines*) Yummy! Yummy! Yummy!
Servant	Broccoli-flavoured jelly?
Guests	Ugh! (*Back to their reading.*)
King	No, thank you, Pritstick! We'll have . . . coconut milk and raspberry juice, mulled wine and best champagne . . .
Guests	(*Looking up from their magazines*) Yummy! Yummy! Yummy! Yummy!
Servant	****-Cola? (*Choose a well-known brand name!*)
Guests	(*Really disgusted!*) Ugh!!! (*Back to their reading.*)
Narrator A	Then the King gave the servant the invitations . . .
	(*The King hands over a set of invitation cards and a list of guests.*)
Narrator B	. . . and a list of guests . . .
Narrator A	. . . and sent him on his way.
	(*Appropriate action. Exit the King. The servant goes along the back of the bench, knocking very deliberately twice on the back of the head of each person in turn. Someone off-stage simultaneously knocks on some wood – imitating a door-knocker – except in the case of the last person in the line, where a bell rings!*)
Servant	(*Knocks*) Invitation . . .
Guest 1	(*Turning round*) For me?
Servant	From the King . . .
Guest 1	Oh, wonderful! (*Accepts the invitation, turns back again and continues reading.*)
Servant	(*Knocks*) Invitation . . .
Guest 1	(*Turning round*) For me?
Servant	From the King . . .
Guest 2	Oh, marvellous! (*Accepts the invitation, turns back again and continues reading.*)
Servant	(*Knocks*) Invitation . . .
Guest 3	(*Turning round*) For me?
Servant	From the King . . .
Guest 3	Oh, fabulous! (*Accepts the invitation, turns back again and continues reading.*)

Servant	(*Knocks, bell rings*) Invitation . . .
Guest 4	(*Turning round*) For me?
Servant	From the King . . .
Guest 4	Oh, brillo-pads! (*Accepts the invitation, turns back again and continues reading.*)
	(*The servant exits.*)
Narrator B	Two days later . . .
Narrator A	. . . the great day had come.
	(*Enter King.*)
King	The great day has come!
Narrator B	Everything was ready.
King	Everything is ready!
Narrator A	The feast was prepared.
King	The feast is prepared. Pritstick!
	(*Enter Servant.*)
Servant	Yes, Your Majesty?
King	Fetch the guests!
Servant	Yes, Sire.
	(*Exit King. The servant then sets off to visit each guest in turn.*)
Narrator B	The servant went from house to house . . .
Narrator A	. . . to tell the guests that everything was ready . . .
Narrator B	. . . to tell them to come to the feast . . .
Narrator A	. . . but one by one they made excuses . . .
	(*As the servant moves along the back of the line, each guest in turn looks up, offers an excuse, then gets up and leaves.*)
Guest 1	Oh, yes, the invitation from the King . . . but we're having a new carpet fitted today. Twenty pounds a square metre, you know. Sorry, can't come. (*Exit.*)
Guest 2	Oh, yes, the invitation from the King . . . but I've got an appointment this afternoon with my financial adviser. Must sort out my pension. Sorry, can't come. (Exit.)
Guest 3	Oh, yes, the invitation from the King . . . but City are playing at home today. Have to be there to cheer them on. Sorry, can't come. (*Exit.*)
Guest 4	Oh, yes, the invitation from the King . . . but I have to watch *Neighbours* this evening. Never miss it. Sorry, can't come. (*Exit.*)
Narrator B	The servant returned to the King.
	(*Enter the King, meeting the servant.*)
King	So, how many are coming to my feast?
Servant	Um . . . (*checking list, counting*) . . . none.
King	None?
Servant	(*Checking list again*) Yes, Your Majesty, none.

Narrator A	Then the King ordered his servant to go out into the streets and alleyways of the city . . .
	(*Appropriate action – the servant goes off-stage and ushers on various individuals, fitting the descriptions of 'poor, crippled, blind and lame'.*)
Narrator B	. . . and to bring in the poor . . .
Narrator A	. . . and the crippled . . .
Narrator B	. . . and the blind . . .
Narrator A	. . . and the lame.
	(*The King greets each one and hands them a drink.*)
Narrator B	But still there was room at the feast.
Narrator A	So the King told his servant . . .
King	Go out into the country lanes and into the villages, and invite more people to come to my feast.
	(*The servant now goes into the audience and invites further people onto the stage to join the party. These could be individuals planted there or unsuspecting members of the audience!*)
Narrator A	And the servant went.
Narrator B	And the people came.
	(*Appropriate action on stage, as the party assembles: drinks are passed round, hands are shaken, everyone looks happy and excited!*)
Narrator A	And they were greatly blessed to share in the King's feast.
Narrator B	And the King was greatly pleased that his house . . . was full.

THE LOrD'S prayer

Introduction

This piece explores the meaning of the Lord's Prayer. There is a Chorus of about six, including one who acts as the leader. A heckler planted in the audience keeps asking to have the lines of the prayer explained. In addition to the introduction and conclusion there are eight small cameos, used to illustrate each line of the prayer. Depending on the personnel available, these could all be performed by different actors or they could all be covered by a group of about six taking various parts. The suggestions for these cameos may have to be modified or rewritten to suit the age of the performers and the context of the performance. For example, the actual banner headlines suggested for the eighth cameo may be judged to be unsuitable in some circumstances.

In order to make an important point about respecting God's name ('hallowed be thy name'), actual examples of blasphemy are included in the second cameo, with a character misusing 'Good Lord' and 'O my God'. The fact that these may not appear to be particularly shocking demonstrates how commonplace has become the breaking of the commandment to respect the name of God.

Bible base   Matthew 6.9-15; 1 Chronicles 29.11; Psalm 25.2.

Cast   Chorus: a group of about six, including the Leader
Heckler (*in the audience*)
For the eight cameos, the following characters, some of which may be played by the same actors:
First cameo: Dad, Child 1 and Child 2
Second cameo: Persons 1 and 2
Third cameo: A group of about five workers
Fourth cameo: Newsreader
Fifth cameo: Aid-worker, White Child, Black Child
Sixth cameo: Neighbour, Child 1 and Child 2
Seventh cameo: Mum, Child
Eighth cameo: Child 1 and Child 2

The Chorus stands to one side of the stage, leaving room for action. There is a chair centre-stage.

Introduction

Leader	Let us pray. Our Father . . .
Chorus	(*Chanting, without much understanding*) Our Father, who art in heaven, hallowed be thy name. Thy kingdom come, thy will be done, on earth as it is in heaven. Give us this day our daily bread. And forgive us our trespasses, as we forgive those who trespass against us. And lead us not into temptation, but deliver us from evil. For thine is the kingdom, the power and the glory. For ever and ever. Amen.
Heckler	(*From the audience*) Could you do that again, please? In English.
Leader	Yes, sure. Let's pray.
Chorus	(*With understanding, thoughtfully*) Our Father in heaven, may your name be honoured; may your kingdom come; may your will be done, on earth as in heaven. Give us today the food that we need. Forgive us for when we break your laws, as we forgive those who offend us. Do not lead us into temptation, and keep us safe from evil. For the kingdom, the power and the glory are yours, now, and for ever. Amen.
Leader	(*To Heckler*) Better?
Heckler	(*Guardedly*) Yes . . . but I still don't get it.
Leader	OK. We'll explain.

First cameo

Chorus	Our Father in heaven . . .
Leader	Jesus said, when you pray, say:
Chorus	Our Father in heaven.
Leader	Can you imagine a perfect father?
Heckler	Not really.
Leader	I know it's hard, but let's try . . .
	(*Dad enters and sits on the chair, working on his laptop. Child 1 enters.*)
Child 1	Dad, have you got time to help me with this homework?
Dad	Of course. Bring it here.
	(*Child 1 goes across and Dad mimes helping. Child 2 enters.*)
Child 2	(*Excitedly, holding up a certificate*) Dad, I got a 'stificate at school today for swimming 10 metres.
Child 1	Thanks, Dad! (*Exit.*)
Dad	(*To Child 2*) Well done! Let's have a look! Brilliant! I'm proud of you!
	(*Child 2 takes the certificate across and Dad shows a lot of interest. Child 1 enters again as Child 2 exits.*)
Child 1	(*Carrying a broken train-set engine*) Dad, I've broken my engine.
Dad	Bring it here. I'll see if I can fix it.
	(*Child 1 goes across and Dad attends to the engine. Child 2 enters.*)
Child 2	(*Very upset*) Dad, that bully over the road just hit me again.
	(*Child 2 goes across to Dad, who consoles the child.*)
Dad	Come here. Now, you two, come with me. I've got something rather special for you in the other room.

(*Dad and the children exit, Dad with his arm round each one's shoulder.*)

Leader	Jesus could have said, when you pray, say:
Chorus	(*Grandly, dramatically*) Almighty, eternal, sovereign, creator God . . .
Leader	But he said, when you pray, say:
Chorus	(*Simply*) Our Father . . . in heaven.
Leader	(*To Heckler*) Got it?
Heckler	Got it! Next bit?

Second cameo

Chorus	May your name be honoured on earth.

(*Enter Persons 1 and 2. Person 2 sits on the chair. Person 1 walks around as in a hurry, clutching a letter, then stops frantically and looks at watch.*)

Person 1	(*Blaspheming*) Good Lord! What a day!
Person 2	(*Praying*) Good Lord, thank you for this day.
Person 1	(*Looking at the letter and responding with a blasphemy*) O my God, you can't trust anyone! (*Exit, angrily.*)
Person 2	(*Praying*) O my God, I trust in you. (*Exit, calmly.*)
Chorus	May your name be honoured on earth.
Leader	(*To Heckler*) Got it?
Heckler	Got it! Next bit?

Third cameo

Chorus	May your kingdom come on earth.

(*A group of about five workers enters. The workers stand around, reading the* Financial Times, *checking share prices and so on. The Chorus sings twice the first verse of the song 'Seek ye first the kingdom of God and his righteousness' (Karen Lafferty, Copyright © 1972 Maranatha! Music). Initially the workers turn their backs on the Chorus. Then, one by one, they turn and listen, show interest, put away their newspapers, go across, shake the Leader's hand and join in with the singing. When the singing finishes each of the workers gives a hug to one of the Chorus members and exits.*)

Chorus	May your kingdom come on earth.
Leader	(*To Heckler*) Got it?
Heckler	Got it! Next bit?

Fourth cameo

Chorus	May your will be done on earth, as in heaven.
	(*The Newsreader enters and takes the seat centre-stage.*)
Newsreader	Good evening. Here are the news headlines.
Chorus	Bong . . .
Newsreader	Today there was an outbreak of peace in . . . (*mention somewhere in the news where there is currently fighting going on*). All fighting, bloodshed and hatred have come to an end.
Chorus	Bong . . .
Newsreader	Throughout Britain, parents and schoolteachers have been stunned by an epidemic of obedience and good behaviour in their children.
Chorus	Bong . . .
Newsreader	And a survey published today reveals that the qualities that teenagers in Britain value most are kindness, gentleness, generosity, forgiveness, patience and self-control.
Chorus	May your will be done on earth, as in heaven.
Leader	(*To Heckler*) Got it?
Heckler	Got it! Next bit?

Fifth cameo

Chorus	Give us today the food that we need.
Heckler	(*Sings*) 'Food, glorious food!' And lots of it, please! Yummy, yummy.
Chorus	Give us today the food that we need.
Leader	The word is 'need' . . .
Chorus	Not 'greed'!

(*An aid-worker enters and takes the chair. As the aid-worker speaks, two children enter from opposite sides of the stage. One is a white child, representing Western greed, carrying a paper bag containing a cream doughnut. The other is a black child, as waif-like as possible, representing African poverty. The Western child unwraps the doughnut, throws the wrapper on the floor and eats the doughnut greedily and messily. Their paths cross and the Western child exits. The African child stops, turns to look at the discarded paper bag, walks back and looks inside it, but it is empty. The child discards the bag and exits.*)

Aid-worker	In the affluent countries of the Western world, one of the biggest threats to health is overeating. In many countries in Africa the biggest threat to health is malnutrition. In today's world, Western greed continues alongside Third World need. (*Exit, after the children.*)
Chorus	Give us today the food that we need.
Heckler	Need, not greed. Got it! Next bit?

Sixth cameo

Chorus	Forgive us for when we break your laws, as we forgive those who offend us.
	(*The Neighbour enters and kneels against the chair, praying.*)
Neighbour	God in heaven, please forgive me this day for my greed and selfishness, for coveting Mr Jones's new car, and for stealing some paper clips from the office at work . . .
	(*A large ball is thrown from off-stage and hits the Neighbour.*)
Neighbour	I don't believe it!
	(*The Neighbour gets up and picks up the ball, looking very cross. Two children enter nervously.*)
Child 1	We're ever so sorry.
Child 2	Can we have our ball back, please?
Neighbour	(*Angry*) I told you yesterday! If your ball lands in my garden again, you lose it! So, that's it!
Child 1	But, we're really, really sorry.
Child 2	Please forgive us!
Neighbour	I've warned you enough times. You don't deserve to be forgiven. Now clear off and leave me in peace!
	(*The children exit, in tears, one way; the Neighbour starts to exit the other way, clutching the ball, but stops as the Chorus speaks . . .*)
Chorus	Forgive us for when we break your laws . . . as we forgive those who offend us.
	(*The Neighbour turns, calls out in the direction of the children, and then exits that way.*)
Neighbour	Um . . . wait a moment . . .
Leader	(*To Heckler*) Got it?
Heckler	Got it! Next bit?

Seventh cameo

Chorus	Do not lead us into temptation.
	(*Mum enters and takes the seat. She is reading a book. Child enters.*)
Mum	Would you just pop and get me an evening paper? Here's the 40 pence. (*Hands money to Child.*)
Child	OK, Mum. Won't be long.
	(*The Vendor enters and meets Child at the edge of the stage.*)
Vendor	(*Calling out something totally unintelligible, along the lines of 'Get your evening news here!'*) Gerriyooreevninoozzah!
Child	Evening paper, please.
Vendor	(*Doing the necessary transaction*) There you go. Only 20p today. Special offer. (*Calling again*) Gerriyooreevninoozzah! (*Exit.*)
	(*Child takes the paper to Mum and hands it over.*)
Child	There you are, Mum. Your evening paper. (*Hesitates, thinking about the 20p change.*)
Mum	Thanks.

Chorus	Do not lead us into temptation.
Child	Um, and, um, oh, by the way . . . there was 20p change today. Special offer. (*Goes to hand over the change.*)
Mum	That's good! Thank you. (*Standing*) But why don't you keep that?
Child	Cor! Thanks, Mum!
	(*They exit.*)
Leader	(*To Heckler*) Got it?
Heckler	Got it! Next bit?

Eighth cameo

Chorus	And keep us safe from evil.

(*Child 1 and Child 2 enter and place a large flip-chart on the chair, where it can be clearly seen by the audience. As they deliver their lines, they turn over or tear off sheets of paper revealing a series of banner headlines: CONCERN ABOUT INCREASE IN CHILD ABUSE; ILLEGAL DRUGS FOUND IN PRIMARY SCHOOLS; TEENAGE DRUNKENNESS ON THE INCREASE; 12-YEAR-OLD GIRL RAPED ON WAY TO SCHOOL; HUNDREDS HURT IN SOCCER GANG WARFARE; KIDS DOWNLOAD NASTY STUFF FROM INTERNET; PARENTS WHO TEACH CHILDREN TO SHOPLIFT; and so on . . .*)

Child 1	Ladies and gentlemen . . .
Child 2	Mums and Dads . . .
Child 1	This is the world . . .
Child 2	. . . where we have to grow up . . .
Child 1	. . . where we have to survive . . .
Child 2	. . . and live our lives . . .
Child 1	. . . and follow God's way.
Child 2	Pray for us.
Child 1	Thank you.
	(*Exit Child 1 and Child 2.*)
Chorus	And keep us safe from evil.
Leader	(*To Heckler, with a more serious tone*) Got it?
Heckler	(*Subdued*) Got it. (*Pause*) Last bit?

Conclusion

Chorus	For the kingdom, the power and the glory are yours.
	(*The Leader moves to centre-stage. The rest of the Chorus kneels.*)
Leader	God is our King!
Chorus	We will serve him.
Leader	God is all-powerful!
Chorus	We will trust him.
Leader	Give God the glory!
Chorus	We will praise him.
Leader	Now and for ever.
Chorus	For the kingdom, the power and the glory are yours, now and for ever. Amen.

THE ANSWER LIES IN THE SOIL

Introduction

This is a version of the parable of the sower and the seed. It should really be called the parable of the different kinds of soil, because the focus of the story that Jesus told is on the different ways in which we can respond to the word of God. I have chosen to present the text of the parable here in the form of rhyming couplets ('doggerel' might be a more accurate description). Used occasionally, this can be an amusing and effective medium for supporting the acting-out of a story in mime.

Two good readers who can clearly emphasize the key words are needed for the narrators who read the verses. They will also require a good sense of timing and some initiative, to link their words with the on-stage actions. Otherwise, depending on the space available, there is potential for a large cast of seeds, weeds, ramblers and stagehands, as well as one crow and the farmer. The text assumes that the farmer is male, but this is not essential; if a female farmer is used, change 'he' and 'his' to 'she' and 'her'. Some imitation rocks will be required, as well as a sun on a pole, a sack of seed, some sweetcorn cobs (seeds still attached!), a large Bible and a range of appropriate costumes, as indicated in the cast list below.

Bible base	Matthew 13.1-9,18-23.
Cast	Farmer Jones
	A crow (*in appropriate costume*)
	Three or four stagehands
	A group of ramblers in boots and anoraks (*these could be the stagehands*)
	A minimum of eight seeds (*small children*); the seeds who will occupy Strip D should have sweetcorn cobs hidden in their pockets
	A minimum of two weeds (*but more if possible*), in appropriate costume

The area of the stage has to be divided into four strips, running from one side of the stage to the other. These represent the four types of soil: the strip nearest the audience (Strip A) is the path, the next (Strip B) is the stony ground, the next (Strip C) is the ground infested with weeds, and the final strip (Strip D) is the good soil. The two Narrators should be off-stage, but visible to the audience.

Dialogue	Stage directions
Narrator 1 When Farmer Jones surveyed his land he found it easy to understand why seed that came from a first-rate shop sometimes produced a third-rate crop.	*Farmer Jones enters and surveys the stage area. He walks around studying his land.*
Narrator 2 Along the front a footpath lay; an unlikely stretch of hardened clay. Any sign of green-leafed shoots had been destroyed by ramblers' boots.	*Farmer Jones comes to the front and indicates Strip A.*
Ramblers (*Singing*) I love to go a-wandering along the farmer's track, and as I go I love to wear my boots and anorak.	*The Ramblers enter. They march across the stage along Strip A, singing. They push past the Farmer and exit briskly.*
Narrator 1 Beyond the path some rocky ground with very shallow soil is found; huge rocks and stones and lumps of granite . . .	*Farmer Jones indicates Strip B.* *Stagehands march on, distribute 'rocks' along Strip B and exit.*
Narrator 2 . . . like somewhere on another planet! Next a strip of land is found where many kinds of weed abound:	*Farmer Jones indicates Strip C.*

Narrator 1
(*Quickly*) Mayweed, fireweed, rockweed,
    chickweed, milkweed, bindweed,
    pokeweed, stickweed,
	A number of children dressed as 'weeds' now enter and position themselves along Strip C.

Narrator 2
(*Quickly*) Knapweed, goutweed,
    thimbleweed, hogweed, ragweed,
    knotweed, tumbleweed, dogweed.
	The 'weeds' sit on the ground and curl up as small as they can.

Narrator 1 (*Very matter-of-fact*) And stinging nettles.	

Narrator 2
Finally, along the back,
away from the weeds and rocks and track,
the farmer likes to look around
this lovely stretch of fertile ground.

Narrator 1
And now, with winter finally going,
the time has come to do his sowing.
At sunrise Farmer Jones is found
scattering all the seed around.

Narrator 2
The wind picks up and blows the seeds
along the path, and in the weeds.
Among the rocks some have ended –
while some at least go where intended.

Narrator 1
The story Jesus told now traces
the fate of the seed in these four places.

Narrator 2
First, the seed that left the sack
to lie exposed upon the track.

Narrator 1
Watching the farmer come and go,
up in a tree, a large, black crow –
seeing the chance for a tasty snack –
swoops down and lands upon the track.
The seed is gobbled up and gone.

Narrator 2
And that is that. (*Pause*) So, let's move on.
Now – bless their little cotton socks –
what chance the seed that's in the rocks?

Narrator 1
At first they quickly start to grow,
but when the sun comes out – oh, no!
The soil is shallow, hard and dry,
and the plants just shrivel up and die.

Narrator 2
So those whose roots did not go deep
were destined for the compost heap.

Farmer Jones indicates Strip D.
He exits.

Farmer Jones re-enters with a sack of seed labelled 'GOOD SEED' and walks along Strip A, miming appropriately. He exits.

The children representing seeds swoop on stage and distribute themselves equally across the four strips. They curl up on the ground as tightly as possible.

The seeds in Strip A give a little wave to identify themselves.

Enter a crow.
The crow swoops onto Strip A and looks hungrily at the seeds there. Exit seeds pursued by crow.

The seeds in Strip B give a little wave to identify themselves.

The seeds in Strip B mime growing quickly. A stagehand walks behind them carrying a sun on a pole. The plants struggle, then wilt.

Farmer Jones and the stagehands drag the seeds in Strip B off-stage.

Narrator 1
What chance that those amongst the weed
might be the ones that will succeed?

*The seeds in Strip C give a little wave
to identify themselves.*

Narrator 2
These seeds find space to put their roots,
and soon we see their new-grown shoots.
But this ground by weeds is occupied,
and they have plans for herbicide!

*The seeds in Strip C gradually grow.
Then the weeds grow alongside them.
The weeds turn and look menacingly
at the other plants.*

Narrator 1
The new-grown plants are crowded out;
the weeds are choking them, no doubt!
They droop, they fade, their leaves turn
　　brown;
they're crumpling up and falling down.

*The weeds now act as though choking
the other plants, who mime the actions
described and collapse in a crumpled heap.
The weeds punch the air victoriously.*

Narrator 2
So those without the space to grow
soon lose the plot – and have to go.

Narrator 1
(*Looking at the weeds; in ordinary
speech, not rhyme*)
Anyone got any weedkiller?
Aha!
Thank you.

*Farmer Jones enters with an aerosol spray.
All the occupants of Strip C exit in
a hurry.*

Narrator 2
Our poor old farmer feels bereft;
but maybe from the seed that's left
the combine harvester will fetch
even more corn than is in this sketch.

*Farmer Jones looks around, disappointed.
He exits. The seeds in Strip D give
a little wave to identify themselves.*

Narrator 1
With a bit of tender loving care,
and the rich and fertile soil down there,
the seeds take root and start to grow.
And then the plants begin to show.

*Farmer Jones returns with a watering-
can and 'waters' the seeds in Strip D.
Farmer exits. Plants grow gradually.*

Narrator 2
So once again within this field
God's miracle is now revealed,
as good seed sown in fertile seams
produces a crop beyond our dreams.

*Plants now come to their full height.
They produce the sweetcorn cobs
from their pockets and hold them
above their heads.*

Narrator 1
God's word is represented here
by the good seed scattered everywhere.
So the question for us would seem to be:
what kind of soil are you and me?

Farmer Jones now returns carrying a large Bible and stands centre-stage, facing the audience, as though reading to them from the Bible.

Narrator 2
Like the path that lost the seed to the bird,
are we hard and resistant to God's word?

Farmer Jones indicates Strip A.

Narrator 1
Or are we like the stony ground,
where only a shallow response is found?

The Farmer steps back and indicates Strip B.

Narrator 2
Are we so busy with our own desires
that the word is choked and then expires?

The Farmer steps back and indicates Strip C.

Narrator 1
Jesus said: 'Be fertile land!
Receive God's word and understand.
New life and joy it will impart
when you take it deep into your heart.'

The Farmer gestures towards Strip D, then returns to the front of the stage and offers up the open Bible to the audience.

WHINGEDOG

Introduction

This sketch is based on the idea of a television consumer programme, like *Watchdog*. It explores the saying of Jesus about not trying to patch up old garments with new cloth. There are ten speaking parts, but, provided there is space, other performers can be involved as various TV studio personnel.

Bible base	Mark 2.21-2; 1 Corinthians 5.7; 2 Corinthians 5.17; Ephesians 4.22-4; Revelation 21.5.
Cast	Readers 1 and 2, to introduce and close the sketch Jules and Ffion, presenters of the TV show *Whingedog* Mr Spatchett Miss Cratchett Mr and Mrs Hatchett Mr Patchit, the spokesman for Universal Patchit dot com Dr Wise, an expert Various TV studio personnel

Jules and Ffion are seated at a desk to one side of the stage. On the other side of the stage is a table with two chairs, where guests will sit and place the objects they bring with them. To add atmosphere and to involve a larger number of players, incorporate various other non-speaking TV personnel: camera operator, sound technician, people answering telephones in the background and so on. The Reader enters, delivers the opening line from centre-stage, then exits.

Reader	Jesus said, 'No-one would sew a patch of unshrunk cloth on an old garment. (*Pause*) If they did . . .' (*Gestures towards Jules and Ffion and exits.*)
Jules	Good evening, viewers, and welcome to this week's edition of *Whingedog*.
Ffion	The consumer programme that gives you the chance to whinge about poor service . . .
Jules	. . . to complain about faulty products . . .
Ffion	. . . to moan about low quality . . .
Jules	. . . and to expose the rip-off merchants and cowboys. Ffion, what do we have to whinge about this evening?
Ffion	Well, Jules, tonight we're doing an exposé of an online Internet service called Universal Patchit dot com.
Jules	Sounds intriguing. So, what does this Universal Patchit dot com do?
Ffion	Well, their website claims that they can supply a patch to repair anything. But let's see what some of our viewers say. Here's a Mr Spatchett from Hertfordshire.

(Enter Mr Spatchett, clutching an old car radiator. He sits at the table and puts the radiator down in front of him.)

Jules	What was your experience of Universal Patchit, Mr Spatchett?
Spatchett	I bought a patch from Universal Patchit dot com to repair the radiator on my car.
Jules	And did it work?
Spatchett	Oh yeah, it was great . . . for about ten minutes. But then the radiator got hot, the patch came off, the hole was worse, and the engine got overheated and exploded.
Jules	So, where did this happen?
Spatchett	On the M25.
Jules	And did you have to abandon your car on the hard shoulder?
Spatchett	Well, some of it. The rest was sort of spread across Hertfordshire.
Ffion	Thank you. So Mr Spatchett's Universal Patchit patch didn't come up to scratch. Who else do we have?

(Exit Mr Spatchett, leaving the radiator on the table. Enter Miss Cratchett, who sits and places an old trainer on the table.)

Jules	Well, this is a Miss Cratchett from Norfolk.
Ffion	What was your experience of Universal Patchit, Miss Cratchett?
Cratchett	I had this hole in one of my expensive designer-label trainers. So I ordered a patch from Universal Patchit dot com, and stuck it on as per the instructions on the packet.
Ffion	And what happened when you put your foot in it, Miss Cratchett?
Cratchett	It was OK to start with, but as soon as I started running, the patch came off, taking half the sole with it.

(She pokes her finger through a hole in the sole of the trainer to demonstrate.)

Jules	Poor sole.
Ffion	Thank you. So, the patch that Universal Patchit dispatched and Miss Cratchett attached was soon detached.

(Exit Miss Cratchett, leaving the trainer on the table. Enter Mr and Mrs Hatchett, who now sit at the table. From the front they appear well dressed – make sure their rears are hidden!)

Jules	Now we have Mr and Mrs Hatchett from Liverpool. You've been using Universal Patchit dot com to repair your clothes, is that right?
Mr H	'A Universal patch will make a perfect match.' That's what it said.
Mrs H	Yeah, it was his idea. Patch up our old clothes, he said. Save money.

(An argument develops. The presenters are left helpless, unable to get a word in.)

Mr H	My idea? I only suggested it. It was your idea to go ahead.
Mrs H	No, it wasn't, it was yours, you old skinflint.
Mr H	When did you ever let me decide anything?
Mrs H	You wait till I get you home.

Mr H	Right, that's it. I'm going.
	(*He gets up to leave.*)
Mrs H	(*Leaving as well*) You're not leaving me here on my own!
	(*As they leave, their back views – with ludicrous patches hanging off their clothes – are revealed to the audience.*)
Ffion	Well, that's certainly one case where the Universal Patchit patch did not make a perfect match.
	(*Mr Patchit enters and sits at the table. Jules interviews him, but never lets him complete a sentence.*)
Jules	Now, we have here a spokesman from Universal Patchit dot com. Mr Patchit, what do you have to say to our viewers who've tried your products?
Patchit	Our company policy is always to offer . . .
Jules	Yes, that's all very well, but is your patch up to scratch?
Patchit	Our product is scientifically tested and . . .
Jules	(*Holding up a piece of paper*) This is a list of government-approved specifications for adhesive products; can you match it, Mr Patchit?
Patchit	Our adhesives are guaranteed for . . .
Jules	Thank you, Mr Patchit. Ffion . . .
	(*An assistant ushers him out, protesting. Dr Wise enters and sits at the table, examining the radiator and trainer.*)
Ffion	Now, here we have our consumer expert to give us his words of wisdom. Dr Wise, what do you make of Universal Patchit dot com?
Dr Wise	Well, Ffion, when something's in as much of a mess as these items here, you have to start again.
Ffion	What, buy new?
Dr Wise	Yes, when things are this bad, you have to go for new. You can't just go on and on patching up the old. You need a completely new start. My advice for your viewers is to stop patching up hopeless causes. Get rid of the old and go for a new start, with a brand-new, good-quality product – one that will last!
Jules	Thank you. Wise words there from Dr Wise.
Ffion	Right, our time is up, so we'll see you all again next week for another edition of *Whingedog*. Goodnight.
Jules	Goodnight.
	(*All freeze. The Readers enter and stand centre-stage.*)
Reader 1	Jesus said: 'No-one would sew a patch of unshrunk cloth on an old garment. If they do, the new piece will pull away from the old, making the tear worse.'
Reader 2	The apostle Paul said: 'Put off your old self . . . be made new in the attitudes of your minds . . . put on the new self, created to be like God in true righteousness and holiness.'
Reader 1	The Lord Jesus said: 'Behold, I am making all things new.'

BEATITUDES AND ATTITUDES

Introduction

This simple and highly structured piece contrasts some of the world's attitudes with the 'beatitudes' of the Lord Jesus, from the sermon on the mount. It requires a leader and a small chorus, who recite the words of the beatitudes; eight other persons whose attitudes contrast with these; and one praying Christian believer, who represents someone trying to put Christ's teaching into practice. (Note that, for the purpose of this piece of drama, I have chosen to interpret the statement 'Blessed are those that mourn, for they will be comforted' in terms of mourning over our sin and the comfort that comes from God's forgiveness. Many commentators take the view that the statement could at least include this meaning.)

Bible base	Matthew 5.1-12.
Cast	Leader Chorus Believer (*a praying Christian*) Persons A, B, C, D, E, F, G, H

Persons A–H are distributed around the stage, facing away from the audience. In turn, they face the audience to deliver their lines, forcefully and in a very self-opinionated manner. They react scornfully to the words of Jesus and the values encapsulated in his teaching, and then turn away again. The Chorus stands to one side, so that it does not obscure the minimal action on stage. The Leader can stand to the front of the stage on the side of the Chorus. On the opposite side of the stage is a Christian believer. This person is kneeling and praying throughout the sketch.

Person A	(*Turning round to face the audience*) I am a self-made man. If you want to be a success like me, you have to learn that in this life you don't get no help from no-one. It's all up to you.
Leader	But Jesus said . . .
Chorus	Blessed are the poor in spirit, for theirs is the kingdom of heaven.
Believer	Lord, in my weakness, I trust in your strength.
Person A	(*Scornful*) I didn't get where I am today by being poor in spirit. (*Turns away from the audience again.*)
Leader	But the kingdom of heaven belongs to them.
Person B	(*Turning round to face the audience*) 'Sorry' is not my favourite word. You won't catch me crying over spilt milk. Life's too short to worry about your mistakes.

Leader	But Jesus said . . .
Chorus	Blessed are those who mourn, for they will be comforted.
Believer	Lord, I am truly sorry for what I have done wrong. In your mercy, forgive me.
Person B	(*Scornful*) I didn't get where I am today by being sorry. (*Turns away from the audience again.*)
Leader	But it is they who will be comforted.
Person C	(*Turning round to face the audience*) I always say you have to look after number one. Stand up for your rights. Don't let no-one push you around.
Leader	But Jesus said . . .
Chorus	Blessed are the meek, for they will inherit the earth.
Believer	Lord, help me to put the interests of others before my own.
Person C	(*Scornful*) I didn't get where I am today by being meek. (*Turns away from the audience again.*)
Leader	But it is they who will inherit the earth.
Person D	(*Turning round to face the audience*) What I think is this. You have to make up your mind what you want out of life – property, money, success – and go all out to get it.
Leader	But Jesus said . . .
Chorus	Blessed are those who hunger and thirst for righteousness, for they will be filled.
Believer	Lord, what I want most of all is to live the kind of life that pleases you.
Person D	(*Scornful*) I didn't get where I am today by hungering and thirsting for righteousness. (*Turns away from the audience again.*)
Leader	But it is they who will be filled.
Person E	(*Turning round to face the audience*) You have to be hard if you want to get on in this life. Don't trust no-one and make sure you get all that's due to you.
Leader	But Jesus said . . .
Chorus	Blessed are the merciful, for they will be shown mercy.
Believer	Lord, help me to forgive others, as you forgive me.
Person E	(*Scornful*) I didn't get where I am today by being merciful. (*Turns away from the audience again.*)
Leader	But it is they who will be shown mercy.
Person F	(*Turning round to face the audience*) A little dishonesty here and there does no-one any harm. Just make sure you don't get found out.
Leader	But Jesus said . . .
Chorus	Blessed are the pure in heart, for they will see God.
Believer	Change my heart, O Lord. Make my motives pure.
Person F	(*Scornful*) I didn't get where I am today by being pure in heart. (*Turns away from the audience again.*)
Leader	But it is they who will see God.

Person G	(*Turning round to face the audience*) I don't mind a bit of aggro. You have to be prepared to fight for what you want.
Leader	But Jesus said . . .
Chorus	Blessed are the peacemakers, for they will be called children of God.
Believer	Lord, help me to bring your peace to this troubled world.
Person G	(*Scornful*) I didn't get where I am today by being a peacemaker. (*Turns away from the audience again.*)
Leader	But it is they who will be called God's children.
Person H	(*Turning round to face the audience*) If you want my opinion, people who go to church or Sunday School are a bunch of wets. I despise people who call themselves Christians.
Leader	But Jesus said . . .
Chorus	Blessed are those who are persecuted because of righteousness, for theirs is the kingdom of heaven.
Person H	(*Scornful*) Hypocrites, the lot of them! (*Turns away from the audience again.*)
	(*Praying Believer raises head and looks towards the Leader, as though distressed by these insults.*)
Leader	Jesus said: 'Blessed are you when people insult you, persecute you and falsely say all kinds of evil against you because of me. Rejoice and be glad, because great is your reward in heaven.'
	(*Persons A, B, C, D, E, F, G and H all turn round to face the audience and speak in unison.*)
Persons A–H	We didn't get where we are today by worrying about . . . heaven!
	(*They all exit briskly. Person A stops just before leaving the stage and turns back towards the audience.*)
Person A	Take it from me. Anyone who lived their life like that (*pointing in the direction of the praying Believer*) . . . well . . . in today's world . . . they'd be crucified. (*Exit.*)

THE LORD LOOKS AT THE HEART

Introduction

This sketch recounts the story of Samuel anointing David as King of Israel. The message is clear and direct, as Samuel himself put it: 'Man looks on the outward appearance, but the Lord looks at the heart.' This is a revised version of a sketch that was first published in *Sketches from Scripture* (National Society/Church House Publishing, 1992). I have reworked it here because that book is now out of print and the sketch is an enjoyable and effective one to put on with a group of youngsters. It is a straightforward piece that provides an opportunity for all available performers to participate. There is a chorus, which should work hard in practice to get the repeated sequence very rhythmical, synchronized and full of expression. The sketch relies on this repetition for its impact as, one after the other, the sons of Jesse are considered and rejected. Two capable actors are required for Jesse and Samuel in particular.

Bible base	1 Samuel 16.1-13.
Cast	The prophet Samuel
	Jesse
	David
	Six other sons and one daughter
	Additional members of the Chorus

All performers, except Jesse, David and Samuel, form the Chorus. They are arranged in an arc facing the audience. There is a box on-stage. Samuel enters and addresses the audience.

Samuel	I am Samuel, the prophet. Only a small prophet, but blame the recession. The Lord has sent me here to Bethlehem, to the home of Jesse.
	(*Jesse enters as his name is mentioned and Samuel gestures towards him.*)
	The Lord has chosen one of Jesse's sons to be the next King of Israel.
Chorus	(*In awe*) The next King of Israel!
Samuel	(*To Jesse*) One of your sons is to be anointed. As the next King of Israel.
Chorus	(*Louder*) The next King of Israel!
Jesse	(*Calling*) Number one son! Step forward please.
	(*Number one son steps forward; for extra humour use a short performer for this part.*)
	Is this the one? (*Pointing*) The next King of Israel?
Chorus	The next King of Israel?

Jesse	A fine young man. Handsome. Tall.
	(*Number one son gets up onto the box.*)
Chorus	(*Raising open hands to their faces*) Handsome. (*Raising one hand to indicate height*) Tall.
Jesse	He must be the one.
Chorus	(*To Samuel, while pointing to number one son*) Is he the one?
Samuel	Well . . .
Chorus	Yes?
Samuel	Perhaps . . .
Chorus	(*Louder and higher*) Yes?
Samuel	Maybe . . .
Chorus	(*Even louder and higher*) Yes?
Samuel	No!
Chorus	No?
Samuel	No!
Chorus	(*Disappointed*) Oh!
	(*Number one son returns to the Chorus, dejected.*)
Jesse	(*Calling*) Number two son! Step forward please.
	(*Number two son steps forward. He gets out his wallet, removes a wad of notes and starts counting them.*)
	Is this the one? (*Pointing*) The next King of Israel?
Chorus	The next King of Israel?
Jesse	A business man. Successful. Ambitious. Rich.
Chorus	(*With an appropriate gesture*) Loads-a-shekels.
Jesse	He must be the one.
Chorus	(*To Samuel, while pointing to number two son*) Is he the one?
Samuel	Well . . .
Chorus	Yes?
Samuel	Perhaps . . .
Chorus	(*Louder and higher*) Yes?
Samuel	Maybe . . .
Chorus	(*Even louder and higher*) Yes?
Samuel	No!
Chorus	No?
Samuel	No!
Chorus	(*Disappointed*) Oh!
	(*Number two son returns to the Chorus, dejected.*)
Jesse	(*Calling*) Number three son! Step forward please.
	(*Number three son steps forward. He is dressed in trendy clothes.*)
	Is this the one? (*Pointing*) The next King of Israel?
Chorus	The next King of Israel?
Jesse	Trendy dresser. Lots of style. Classy clothes. Impressive or what?

Chorus	Dig those Levis, Sammy-baby.
Jesse	He must be the one.
Chorus	(*To Samuel, while pointing to number three son*) Is he the one?
Samuel	Well . . .
Chorus	Yes?
Samuel	Perhaps . . .
Chorus	(*Louder and higher*) Yes?
Samuel	Maybe . . .
Chorus	(*Even louder and higher*) Yes?
Samuel	No!
Chorus	No?
Samuel	No!
Chorus	(*Disappointed*) Oh!
	(*Number three son returns to the Chorus, dejected.*)
Jesse	(*Calling, but beginning to sound a little fed up*) Number four son! Step forward please.
	(*Number four son steps forward. He is dressed in a football strip.*)
	Is this the one? (*Pointing*) The next King of Israel?
Chorus	The next King of Israel?
Jesse	First-class sportsman. Premier striker. Our leading goal-scorer.
	(*Someone from the front row of the audience tosses a football onto the head of the son, who heads it back.*)
Chorus	Goal! (*Follow this with a local football chant.*)
Jesse	He must be the one.
Chorus	(*To Samuel, while pointing to number four son*) Is he the one?
Samuel	Well . . .
Chorus	Yes?
Samuel	Perhaps . . .
Chorus	(*Louder and higher*) Yes?
Samuel	Maybe . . .
Chorus	(*Even louder and higher*) Yes?
Samuel	No!
Chorus	No?
Samuel	No!
Chorus	(*Disappointed*) Oh!
	(*Number four son returns to the Chorus, dejected.*)
Jesse	(*Calling, but sounding even more fed up*) Number five son! Step forward please.
	(*Number five son steps forward. He is carrying a book labelled something like* Advanced Mathematics.)
	Is this the one? (*Pointing*) The next King of Israel?
Chorus	The next King of Israel?

Jesse	The brains of the family. Twelve GCSEs. A-star grades. Knows his tables backwards.
Samuel	Really? (*To number five son*) What's five times seven?
No. 5 Son	Fifty-three.
Chorus	See what we mean?
Jesse	He must be the one.
Chorus	(*To Samuel, while pointing to number five son*) Is he the one?
Samuel	Well . . .
Chorus	Yes?
Samuel	Perhaps . . .
Chorus	(*Louder and higher*) Yes?
Samuel	Maybe . . .
Chorus	(*Even louder and higher*) Yes?
Samuel	No!
Chorus	No?
Samuel	No!
Chorus	(*Disappointed*) Oh!
	(*Number five son returns to the Chorus, dejected.*)
Jesse	(*Calling, now sounding desperate!*) Number six son. Step forward please.
	(*Number six son steps forward. He is wearing a vest, with his arms exposed. He flexes his muscles.*)
	Is this the one? (*Pointing*) The next King of Israel?
Chorus	The next King of Israel?
Jesse	The strong man in the family. Just watch this.
	(*Jesse hands number six son a 'doctored' telephone directory, which he easily tears in half, in an arrogant manner.*)
Chorus	Wow! Look at those muscles!
Jesse	He must be the one.
Chorus	(*To Samuel, while pointing to number six son*) Is he the one?
Samuel	Well . . .
Chorus	Yes?
Samuel	Perhaps . . .
Chorus	(*Louder and higher*) Yes?
Samuel	Maybe . . .
Chorus	(*Even louder and higher*) Yes?
Samuel	No!
Chorus	No?
Samuel	No!
Chorus	(*Disappointed*) Oh!
	(*Number six son returns to the Chorus, dejected.*)
Jesse	(*Calling, but sounding optimistic again!*) Number one daughter! Step forward please.

(*His daughter steps forward and curtsies to Samuel.*)
Is this the one? (*Pointing*) The next King of Israel?

Chorus	(*Sounding very doubtful*) The next King of Israel?
Samuel	A girl?
Chorus	Equal opportunities?
Jesse	She could be the one.
Chorus	(*To Samuel, while pointing to the daughter*) Is she the one?
Samuel	No!
Chorus	(*Disappointed*) Oh!

(*The daughter returns to the Chorus, dejected.*)

Samuel	Any more?

(*Jesse counts on his fingers.*)

Jesse	Well, there is David.
Chorus	(*Scornfully*) David! (*They fall about laughing.*)
Jesse	The youngest in the family. He's with the sheep.
Samuel	Bring David here.

(*Jesse exits to fetch David.*)

Jesse	(*Off-stage, calling out*) Da-vid!
David	(*Off-stage, calling out*) Coming, Dad!
Samuel	Remember this. We look at the outward appearance, but the Lord looks at the heart.

(*Jesse returns with David.*)

Samuel	Is this David?
Jesse	This is David, my youngest son, a shepherd-boy.
Chorus	(*With disbelief*) Is he the one?
Samuel	(*Pause; and then . . .*) Yes. He is the one!
Chorus	No!
Samuel	Yes!
Chorus	No!
Samuel	Yes!

(*David kneels. Samuel takes out a small bottle and acts as though anointing him with oil.*)
David, I anoint you. As the next King of Israel.

Chorus and Jesse	(*Kneeling*) The next King of Israel.

WHO WANTS TREASURE IN HEAVEN?

Introduction

This sketch puts the story of the rich young ruler into the format of the popular television game-show *Who Wants to be a Millionaire?* The young man who came to Jesus had inherited a fortune in earthly treasures and now wanted to know how he could inherit eternal life. For him personally – because his riches were so important to him – the answer Jesus gave was that he should give all his money to the poor and follow Jesus. This is the final question posed to the rich young ruler in this sketch. He makes the wrong choice, preferring to try to keep the commandments. So he loses treasure in heaven and goes away sadly.

The sketch has two main performers: Chris, the host, and Rich, the rich young ruler. The amplified voice of the gospel-writer Matthew is heard when Rich decides to phone a friend. In addition there is a group of viewers, who start off as competitors for the first round, and then become the TV audience. This group can be as large as required to involve all available performers. The director of this sketch should ensure that they are familiar with the format of the TV show and then add to the script below all the necessary ingredients of tension; dramatic background music; spotlights and flashing lights; audience reaction; computer screens; interaction between Chris and Rich; the host's mannerisms; and so on.

A Power Point presentation of the questions and answers to accompany this sketch is available, free of charge, from d.haylock@uea.ac.uk

> **Bible base**   Matthew 19.16-26; Mark 10.17-27; Luke 18.18-27.
>
> **Cast**   Chris, the host
> Rich, the competitor
> Matthew (*amplified voice only*)
> A group of viewers

As far as is practicable, try to replicate the setting and atmosphere of the TV show. The viewers are on-stage, seated. They each have a card on which is written the letter B or (in one case only) the letter A. These cards can also be used to represent the keypads that they use in the opening round. Chris enters to a huge round of applause from the viewers.

Chris   Good evening, everyone, and welcome to another edition of *Who Wants Treasure in Heaven?*

(*The viewers applaud again.*)

(*Gesturing towards the viewers*) And here are tonight's group of hopefuls, ready to play 'fastest finger first'. Are you ready? Fingers on your keypads? You know the rules. The fastest competitor gets the chance to go forward to tonight's round of *Who Wants Treasure in Heaven?* So, here's the question. Put these four books that contain the Old Testament law in the order they appear in the Bible: A, Leviticus; B, Numbers; C, Exodus; D, Deuteronomy. Go!

(*The viewers act as though pressing buttons on a computer keypad. After about ten seconds, a buzzer sounds and Chris continues.*)

OK, so here's the right answer: first it's Exodus, then Leviticus, Numbers and finally Deuteronomy. Let's see who got it right . . . only six competitors got it right. And the fastest, in only 3.5 seconds, was Rich! Rich, come over here and join me!

(*Applause. Rich comes across and stands beside Chris, who puts an arm round his shoulder.*)

Bit of an expert in Old Testament law, Rich?

Rich	Studied it all my life, Chris.
Chris	Well done. So, Rich, do you want treasure in heaven?
Rich	Yes, Chris! You bet I do!
Chris	OK, then, here we go. Let's play *Who Wants Treasure in Heaven?*

(*More applause, as they march across to the two chairs and sit facing each other.*)

This is Rich. As you can see he's a young man. His home is in Judaea, where he's well known as one of the local rulers. And you're rich, is that right?

Rich	Yes. My name is Rich.
Chris	I mean, that you, Rich, are actually rich!
Rich	Right. Got you. Oh, yeah. I've inherited quite a bit . . .
Chris	Like, you're already a millionaire? Right?
Rich	Well, yes, actually. But . . . well, money's not everything. There must be more to life than stashing up loads of dosh.
Chris	There certainly is. You can stash up treasure in heaven! Are you ready to play the game?
Rich	Yes, Chris.
Chris	Remember, you've got three lifelines. You can go fifty-fifty; you can ask the audience; and you can phone a friend. OK. Here's your first question to take you onto the first step towards . . . treasure in heaven. Which of the following is *not* true about treasures stored up on earth? A, they will last for ever; B, they can go rusty; C, they can get moth-eaten; D, they can get stolen.
Rich	That's A, Chris: they will last for ever. That's the one that's not true.
Chris	Sure?
Rich	Yes, I'm sure. Some of my stuff's gone rusty and some of it's got moth-eaten! And I know it can get stolen. It's definitely A, Chris.

	Final answer.
Chris	It's the right answer! You're on the first step towards treasure in heaven.
	(He shakes Rich's hand. The viewers applaud.)
	OK, Rich, here's your second question. This will take you to a quarter of the way towards treasure in heaven. The kingdom of heaven is like a wonderful treasure hidden in a field. In the story that Jesus told, what did someone who found this treasure do? A, go home and forget all about it; B, go and buy another field instead; C, sell everything else and buy the field; D, put off thinking about it until later.
Rich	*(Hesitating)* I'm not sure. It might be D. That's what I would do. But it depends . . .
Chris	Take your time. What are you thinking?
Rich	Well, if it was a really wonderful treasure . . . well, I mean, he'd obviously have to sell whatever he had to get it. I think it must be C. Sell everything else and buy the field.
Chris	Are you sure, Rich? Final answer?
Rich	Yes. It must be that. Final answer, Chris.
Chris	Rich . . . *(Mock seriousness)* you were on the first step towards treasure in heaven. *(Pause, and then excitedly)* You're now a quarter of the way there! It's the right answer!
	(He shakes Rich's hand. Rich looks relieved. The viewers applaud.)
Chris	OK, your next question. Get this right and you'll be halfway towards treasure in heaven. Nervous?
Rich	Nervous! I'm terrified!
Chris	Well, take your time, Rich. And remember, you've still got your three lifelines. Here's your next question. Get this right and you're halfway towards treasure in heaven. OK?
Rich	OK, Chris.
Chris	Right. To lead to eternal life, should you follow: A, the narrow path; B, the broad path; C, the M25; or D, the yellow-brick road?
Rich	Mm. Eternal life . . . I ought to know this . . . that's something I'm really interested in. I think I'll take a fifty-fifty, Chris.
Chris	OK. We'll take away two of the wrong answers. There they go. That leaves us with: A, the narrow path; or B, the broad path.
Rich	Mm. I'm still not sure.
Chris	To lead to eternal life, should you follow: A, the narrow path; or B, the broad path? Get this right, Rich, and you're halfway towards treasure in heaven. It's a straight choice. One or the other. One path leads to eternal life, the other does not.
Rich	I think I'll ask the audience.
Chris	OK, audience. Your turn. Let's see if you can get Rich halfway towards treasure in heaven. Make your choice now. A or B?
	(The viewers hold up cards to indicate A or B; all of them except one hold up B.)

Chris	That's ninety-five per cent choosing option B, and only five per cent option A. That's a pretty big majority choosing the broad path, Rich.
	(*The viewers put down their cards.*)
Rich	(*Agonizing a little*) I don't know. I'm not sure it's always the wisest choice to follow the crowd.
Chris	It's your choice, Rich. You have to decide. The narrow path or the broad path . . .
Rich	I'm sure it must be the narrow path. Yes. I'll go for the narrow path.
Chris	You're ignoring the advice of ninety-five per cent of the audience. Confident?
Rich	Yes, I think so. Option A, the narrow path.
Chris	Final answer?
Rich	Final answer.
Chris	Rich. (*Seriously*) You were a quarter of the way towards treasure in heaven. (*Pause*) You've chosen the narrow path. (*Excitedly*) You're now halfway! It's the right answer!
	(*He shakes Rich's hand. Rich looks as though he can't believe it. The viewers applaud enthusiastically.*)
	Phew! Ready for the final question, Rich?
Rich	OK, Chris, let's go for it.
Chris	Right. Now, remember, if you make the right choice on this question, you will have treasure in heaven. You've got one lifeline left: you can phone a friend. So, here we go.
	Rich, you have already inherited a fortune. We know that that inheritance is very important to you. But what must you personally do to inherit eternal life? OK? That's the question: what must you – Rich – do to inherit eternal life? Here are the options: A, be a good citizen and live a decent life; B, go to church every week; C, keep as many of the commandments as you can; or D, give your money to the poor and follow Jesus.
Rich	(*Hesitantly*) I think I know this one. I think it's C. Keep as many of the commandments as you can.
Chris	It's up to you, Rich. Your decision. You can still phone a friend.
Rich	I think I'll do that. Yes, I'll phone a friend.
Chris	Right. Who's your friend, Rich?
Rich	I think I'll phone Matthew.
Chris	Who's Matthew?
Rich	Well, he used to be a tax-collector. But now he's a disciple of Jesus. I think he'll definitely know the answer to this one.
	(*The sound of a telephone ringing is heard.*)
Chris	OK, then. The phone's ringing.
	(*The voice of Matthew is heard, amplified, as though speaking on the telephone to Chris.*)
Matthew	Hello?

Chris	Matthew! Hello, it's Chris here on *Who Wants Treasure in Heaven?*
Matthew	Goodness gracious!
Chris	(*Imitating his response*) Goodness gracious! Matthew, I've got Rich here. He's well on the way towards treasure in heaven. He just lacks one thing. And that's the right answer to the final question. With your help we can get him to make the right choice. OK?
Matthew	I'll do my best, Chris.
Chris	Right, the next voice you hear will be Rich. He'll read you the question and then you have thirty seconds to answer.
Rich	Hi, Matthew. What must I personally do to inherit eternal life? A, be a good citizen and live a decent life; B, go to church every week; C, keep as many of the commandments as I can; or D, give my money to the poor and follow Jesus.
Matthew	It's D, Rich. Definite. Give your money to the poor and follow Jesus.
Rich	(*Worried at this suggestion*) Are you sure?
Matthew	Hundred per cent, Rich.
Rich	(*Disappointed*) OK, thanks, Matthew. Bye.
Chris	Right, Rich. Matthew thinks it's D. You thought it's C. Time for you to decide.
Rich	(*Agonizing*) I don't think I can go for D. Give my money to the poor and follow Jesus? Matthew ought to know what he's talking about, I know . . . but . . . no, that can't be right. I can't do that. That's too much. It's got to be C. That's reasonable, isn't it? Keep as many of the commandments as I can . . .
Chris	Final answer?
Rich	Yes. I've made up my mind. I can't go for D. Final answer. C. Keep as many of the commandments as I can.
Chris	Rich, the question was, how can you personally inherit eternal life? One option was to give your money to the poor and to follow Jesus. But you have decided to hold onto your money and to try to keep as many of the commandments as you can. Rich, you had a million pounds. You've still got a million pounds. But, I'm sorry . . . you've lost treasure in heaven.
	(*Gasps of horror from the viewers. Chris consoles Rich. Rich gets up and, slowly and sadly, walks away.*)

Doing drama too much of a palaver?

Not any more.

Specially written for performance by or to children in school assemblies and family services, these drama items are easy to perform and great to watch. All the titles in our drama series are A4 format and fully photocopiable!

One Cool Cat and other sketches

Derek Haylock   £8.95   ISBN 0 7151 4975 X

Aimed at young people in churches or schools, these sketches have been written to involve a good number of performers with varied acting talent. This lively and humorous collection of creative drama scripts uses a wide variety of styles and settings. All present a clear, biblically-based Christian message.

Acting Up

2ND EDITION

Dave Hopwood

£7.95   0 7151 4970 9

Taking a fresh perspective on well-known Bible stories this collection offers traditional sketches, as well as raps; narrated mimes; response stories (involves audience participation) and entertaining monologues.

A Fistful of Sketches

2ND EDITION

Dave Hopwood

£7.95   0 7151 4969 5

Aimed at teenagers, this book encourages the use of drama amongst teenagers, whether they are performing it, or watching it. It gives tips on setting up your own drama group, preparing for performance and developing drama techniques, as well as 27 sketches, raps, mimes and poems.

The Good Rollerblader and Other Sketches

Instant drama for schools and churches

Jon Webster

£7.95   0 7151 4944 X

Open this book and meet amazing characters like the Good Rollerblader and the Lost Grandchild. Travel around the world through the stories of historical figures like Baboushka and St. Francis.

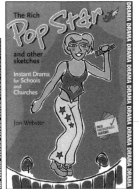

The Rich Pop Star

Instant drama for schools and churches

Jon Webster

£7.95   0 7151 4956 3

The second in Jon Webster's photocopiable series of sketches for use in collective worship and during all-age services.